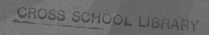

Footprints in the Snow

Counting by Twos

by **Michael Dahl**   illustrated by **Todd Ouren**

Special thanks to our advisers for their expertise:

Stuart Farm, M.Ed., Mathematics Lecturer
University of North Dakota, Grand Forks

Susan Kesselring, M.A., Literacy Educator
Rosemount-Apple Valley-Eagan (Minnesota) School District

PICTURE WINDOW BOOKS
Minneapolis, Minnesota

Managing Editor: Catherine Neitge
Creative Director: Terri Foley
Art Director: Keith Griffin
Editor: Christianne Jones
Designer: Todd Ouren
Page production: Picture Window Books
The illustrations in this book were prepared digitally.

Picture Window Books
5115 Excelsior Boulevard
Suite 232
Minneapolis, MN 55416
877-845-8392
www.picturewindowbooks.com

Printed in the United States of America.

Library of Congress Cataloging-in-Publication Data
Dahl, Michael.
Footprints in the snow : counting by twos / by Michael Dahl;
illustrated By Todd Ouren.
p. cm. — (Know your numbers)
Includes bibliographical references and index.
ISBN 1-4048-0946-5 (hardcover)
1. Counting—Juvenile literature. I. Ouren, Todd, ill. II. Title.

QA113.D329 2004
513.2'11—dc22   2004019582

TWO footprints in the snow,
across the field,
where do they go?

3

FOUR footprints in the snow, down the hill, where do they go?

4

SIX footprints in the snow,
into the woods,
where do they go?

7

EIGHT footprints in the snow,
under the branches,
where do they go?

2 **4** **6** **8**

TEN footprints in the snow,
over the bridge,
where do they go?

2 4 6 8 10

12

TWELVE footprints in the snow, between the bushes, where do they go?

2 4 6 8 10 12 **14**

14

FOURTEEN footprints in the snow,
past the snowmen,
where do they go?

15

2 4 6 8 10 12 14 16

SIXTEEN footprints in the snow,
along the log,
where do they go?

EIGHTEEN footprints in the snow,
behind the berries,
where do they go?

• • •	• • •	• • •	• • •	• • •	• • •	• • •	• • •	• • •
2	**4**	**6**	**8**	**10**	**12**	**14**	**16**	**18**

19

• •	• •	• •	• •	•	•	•	•	•	•
2	**4**	**6**	**8**	**10**	**12**	**14**	**16**	**18**	**20**

20

TWENTY footprints in the snow,
through the gate,
where do they go?

22

Footprints stop outside the door.
Come in! Warm up!
Then we'll go make more!

Fun Facts

The coldest temperature recorded on Earth was minus 129 F (minus 89 C) in Vostok, Antarctica.

Every snowflake has six sides, but no two snowflakes are the same.

Stampede Pass, Washington, is the snow capital of the United States.

Snow is not white. It is clear. It looks white because each snowflake breaks up the sun's light into many colors. Your eyes can't handle that much light and color. That's why you see white.

On the Web

FactHound offers a safe, fun way to find Web sites related to this book. All of the sites on FactHound have been researched by our staff. *www.facthound.com*

1. Visit the FactHound home page.
2. Enter a search word related to this book, or type in this special code: 1404809465
3. Click on the FETCH IT button.

Your trusty FactHound will fetch the best Web sites for you!

24

Find the Numbers

Now you have finished reading the story, but a surprise still awaits you. Hidden in each picture is a multiple of 2 from 2 to 20. Can you find them all?

2–on the squirrel's tail

4–on the bridge

6–on the squirrel

8–the cardinal's feet

10–on the nest

12–in the left bush

14–on the snowman's arm

16–on the log

18–in the bush on the right

20–the gate latch

Look for all of the books in the Know Your Numbers series: